Winning by WAITING

Written by Anastasia Suen

Content Consultant
Taylor K. Barton, LPC
School Counselor

Rourke
Educational Media

rourkeeducationalmedia.com

Scan for Related Titles
and Teacher Resources

www.rourkeeducationalmedia.com

PHOTO CREDITS: Cover: © EHStock; page 4: © Jan Tyler; page 5: © cjp; page 6: © Vstock; page 7: © ktasimarr; page 8, 13: © LifesizeImages; page 9: © goldenangel; page 10: © kali9; page 11: © yenwen; page 12, 15, 21: © asiseeit; page 14: © GlobalStock; page 17: © MBI_Images; page 18: © Marilyn Nieves; page: 19: © Maica; page 20: © JaniceRichard; page 22: © velkol

Edited by Precious McKenzie

Cover and Interior Design by Tara Raymo

Library of Congress PCN Data

Winning by Waiting / Anastasia Suen
(Social Skills)
ISBN 978-1-62169-908-8 (hard cover) (alk. paper)
ISBN 978-1-62169-803-6 (soft cover)
ISBN 978-1-62717-014-7 (e-Book)
Library of Congress Control Number: 2013937303

Rourke Educational Media
Printed in the United States of America,
North Mankato, Minnesota

Also Available as:

rourkeeducationalmedia.com

customersevice@rourkeeducationalmedia.com • PO Box 643328 Vero Beach, Florida 32964

TABLE OF CONTENTS

HOW NATURE CREATES

Let nature show you how to make things grow.

You don't always win by being fast. Sometimes slow is the way to go. Yes, you can win by waiting. How do you know that's true? Go to the window and look outside. Almost everything in the natural world was created the slow way.

You have to wait to see things change. Waiting for something takes **patience**. A small seed takes time to grow into something big. With patience, you experience it for yourself.

Inside seeds are plant powerhouses. Add just a little water, soil, and sunlight.

You can grow plants indoors if you are patient. You'll need to water them regularly and provide sunlight.

You can try it yourself by planting seeds. Plant seeds in the rich soil of your backyard. Or bring nature indoors and plant your seeds in a flowerpot on the windowsill.

Then one day, after all that waiting, it happens. Sprouts pop out of the soil and your seedlings grow into plants. The seeds were growing all that time, you just couldn't see it. Your work and patience paid off!

After you work and wait, your reward comes!

Working and waiting can help you get something new for yourself.

Working and waiting can help you win in other ways. If you want to buy something new, you can work to earn money. There is always work to be done around the house.

It can take a while to earn enough to buy what you really want. You will have to wait until you have saved enough money.

Because you worked hard and saved your money, you could buy something that you really wanted.

PLAN TO PRACTICE

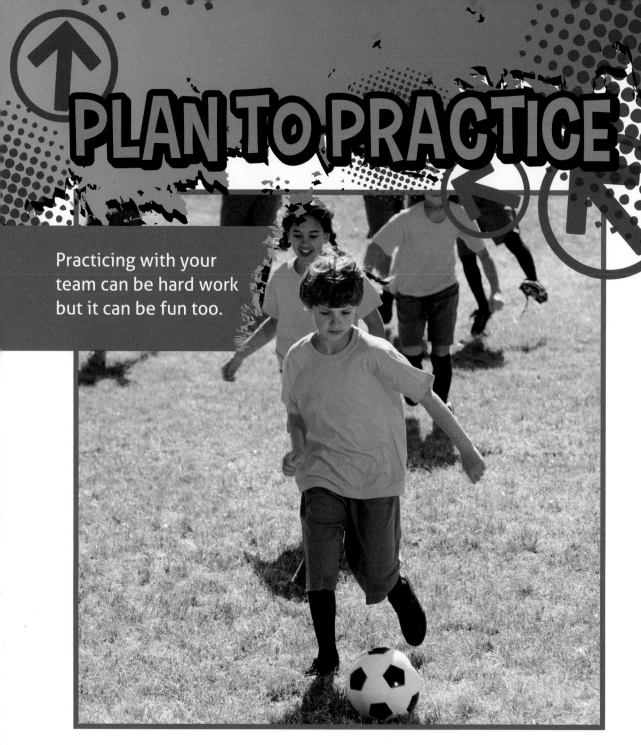

Practicing with your team can be hard work but it can be fun too.

You can win by making a plan. That's how you win in sports. You plan your life so that you have lots of time to practice. If a sport is difficult, you have to **persist** and keep trying. Sometimes it takes persistence to win.

If you play an instrument, practice is important too. Make time in your day to practice so you can improve.

You practice your sport after school. You practice some more on the weekends. You practice your sport with your team once or twice a week. Day by day and week by week, you practice your sport. After a while, all of that practice adds up.

No matter how good you are at a sport, if you want to keep excelling, you must keep practicing.

Spending time practicing is how you **improve** your skills. Just showing up isn't enough to win the game. It takes skill to win when you play sports and you only get that when you practice. Your skill comes because you give yourself time to grow and learn.

You did it! All of that practice paid off!

Each time you play the game, you can get better at it. Each time you practice, you can learn something new. When you give yourself time to grow as a player, you win no matter what the scoreboard says. Becoming a better player is a win you can give yourself.

BREAK YOUR PROJECT INTO STEPS

When planning your project, think of ways you can have fun while you're working on it.

Sometimes you have a big **project** to work on at school. You may have to work with a team. Or you may have to do all of the work by yourself. Either way, making a plan will help you get the project done. Being **organized** is the key to success.

When you find out about a big project, ask when the **deadline** is. Then you can make a plan. Start right away and divide the project up. What do you need to do? Who will work on each step? How long do you have to make everything work?

15

You've worked on projects before so you know the truth. The work you do for a project **rarely** works out the first time. It takes time to figure out what will work.

Be **responsible** and start right away so you can give yourself time to make mistakes. You need time to try out every possibility. You can only find out what will work by trying things out.

You can make it work by going step by step.

When you're working hard, it's important to stop and take a short break.

Starting right away will also give you time to take a break in the middle of your project. After you work on a project for a while, you have filled your mind with ideas about what to do. You may start to feel overwhelmed or confused. When you take a short break, your **subconscious** mind will still be thinking things over.

You can get some great ideas when you exercise!

Taking a break in the middle of your project is the secret to your success. Stop working for a while and do something else. Then when you come back to your project, you'll see it differently. Sometimes you will even figure out the answer when you are doing something else!

REMEMBER TO BREATHE

Many people take time to be quiet at the beginning and the end of the day. They focus on just being alive.

Don't forget to breathe! Remember to stop once or twice a day and wait. Close your eyes and quiet your mind. Don't think about anything. Don't worry about problems. Just listen to yourself breathe. Count your breath as you slowly breathe in and out ten times.

Making time to be quiet and breathe will calm you down. After you wait, you can think clearly. You will know how to solve your problems. You will know what to do next.

You have the power to make things happen. You can be patient with yourself and with others. You can be organized and make a plan. You can be persistent and keep practicing. Yes, you can win by waiting!

GLOSSARY

argument (AR-gyoo-MENT): when people disagree and get upset

deadline (DED-line): the time something is due

improve (in-PROOV): to get better

organized (OR-guh-nized): to make things neat and orderly

patience (PAY-shuhnss): waiting without getting upset

persist (pur-SIST): to keep doing something

project (PROJ-ekt): a school assignment that takes a long time

rarely (RAIR-lee): not very often

responsible (ri-SPON-suh-buhl): in charge of doing something

subconscious (sub-KON-shuhss): the part of your mind where you have thoughts and feelings you are not aware of

INDEX

WEBSITES TO VISIT

singdancelearn.com/character-education-songs/patience-song

havefunteaching.com/songs/character-songs/patience-song

www.humanityquest.com/topic/art_activities/index.asp?theme1=patience

ABOUT THE AUTHOR

Anastasia Suen lives with her family in Plano, Texas. She has quiet time to breathe in the morning, takes exercise breaks, and always uses a calendar to plan her big projects.

Meet The Author!
www.meetREMauthors.com